Praise for *Rights, Wrongs, and In-Betweens*

In "*Rights, Wrongs, and In-Betweens*," Indigo crafts an
intimate journey through the landscape of human connections,
from first love to heartbreak, from letting go to finding oneself.
Through a series of deeply personal letters and confessionals,
Indigo Mapa's debut poetry collection captures the raw emotions
of growing up and the delicate art of healing. Each poem
serves as a dedication—to those who stayed, those who left,
and those who shaped the path to self-discovery. It's exciting
to see Indigo's unique voice emerge, and we are so glad
to have her in the WriteGirl community.

Keren Taylor
Executive Director of WriteGirl

In "Absent," love and abandonment collide, raising questions
about what it means to mourn someone who never stayed,
and why that pain still lingers. Through poems that are by
turns raw, reflective, and resolute, Mapa shows us how to live
in the in-between, and how to write through it.

Shandela Contreras
Award-winning Spoken Word Poet
and Author of *Every Beautiful Pen Bleeds Through*

"Indigo's poems in *Rights, Wrongs and In-Betweens* showcase the writer's voice profoundly. The way and style each poem is written catch the reader's eye immediately. These poems feel as if you're having a conversation with Indigo yourself; that's how personal and intimate these poems get.

Celeste Alyssa Gomez
Author & Owner of *La Poeta Publications*

"Indigo Mapa's *Rights, Wrongs, and In-Betweens* is a stunning exploration of love, desire, home, and coming-of-age experiences. With fierce intensity, she reminisces on loves lost, yearns for the city she lives in, meditates on her own worth and perception of herself. She longs, she yearns, and her words burn the page while moving the reader's heart. This is just the beginning of Mapa's fruitful pursuit of poetry and I'm already excited to see where she takes us next."

Sofía Aguilar,
Author of *amor.*

RIGHTS, WRONGS, AND IN-BETWEENS

INDIGO DHARMA MAPA

Dharma Publishing House
8549 Wilshire Boulevard Unit #1036,
Beverly Hills, California 90211

LCCN: 2025911273
ISBN: 979-8-9990480-0-4 (paperback) |
979-8-9990480-1-1 (ebook)
All rights reserved.
Printed in the United States of America.

Visit the author's site: www.indigomapa.com
Email: idm@indigomapa.com

Editor: Jenesis Fonseca
Cover design & Formatting: Kelly Carter
Author photograph by: Rah-San "Sage" Bailey

For Mom,

I hope I live up to the name you've given me.

ACKNOWLEDGEMENTS

I owe many thanks to those who have taken the time and energy to believe in me and this book. No matter how alone you might feel, someone is always out there to look out for you.

I'd like to thank my mom first and foremost, for she is a constant muse in my life. Every word I write or type will always be dedicated to her.

I'd like to thank Jenesis Fonseca, my editor. Your set of eyes has brought this painting of words to life, I'm forever grateful. You are just as much of a painter as the next.

Thank you to Celeste Gomez for your wise words and mentorship, and for connecting me to the right people; this project would not be as colorful without you.

Special thanks to my friends and family who have inspired me to write truthfully, my feelings for you stay candid and transparent. I hope this book has proved it so, I adore you all as inspirations and as people I can dedicate my words to. You know who you are.

I'd like to thank Auden Wood and Rah-san "Sage" Bailey for bringing my words to life with photographs. I'm forever in debt to your beautiful craft. Thank you for sharing the vision with me.

Thank you to WriteGirl for being my mentors since I was a tween; you've ignited a fire in me that will never cease. Because of you guys, I will use my pen as my sword and my keyboard as my shield.

A special thanks to the ones who broke my heart, I will always have a special place in my heart for mean motherfuckers like you guys. Keep it coming, I'll always have the last word.

Lastly, thank you to whoever reads this book. I hold so much love for the readers and curious individuals who keep art alive, I hope I can keep writing for myself and for you.

I

To
The Ones
Still With
Me...

FOR MOM

I wrote to you an eternity ago. It's not that I didn't want to; I just felt at peace with our relationship. Words of gratitude and affection have never been easier to give. I'm older, maybe wiser, but still not smarter than you. You'll always have this electric intellect that gives you the universe's answers, which I'm still figuring out.

The letters I wrote you when I was younger were apologetic. Maybe we fought, or I did something unexplainably bad. Little did I know that it would be my gift. So, thank you, for a multitude of reasons, but for being the first person I ever wrote to.

When my pen hits the paper or my nails clack on the keyboard, I always have you in mind. For years, I have looked to others to become my muse. When my biggest muse has always been in front of me. You, ma, are beyond remarkable. Resilience and tough grace isn't an easily found balance. I look at you in awe when unapologetic confidence spews out like the hot coffee you brew on our dark magenta Keurig every morning. Law school can be demanding, but it makes me all the more proud of you.

It's damn near impossible to ignore the titan of a speaker you are. Despite ALWAYS being spread too thin, you're always giving your all. No amount of Batgirls, Amazonians–hell, all the heroes can compare to you. You are clarity and assurance incarnated, a fire so bright that you simply cannot be ignored.

This letter isn't from daughter to mother, but rather from human to human.

I'm grateful and forever lucky to call you the one who birthed me, but… if we were strangers in another life, I know I'd love you all the same. When I'm lost in this hellish maze we laugh at called life, one direction I know to head into is towards you.

I'll forever gloat and sing praises of you being my mother. You are my best friend. I hope we'll always fight, grab brunch, sing to boy bands, be your permanent passenger, your sister, and your daughter. When people see us together, I hope they think of their own moms and daughters. I hope they grovel and cry to them so they can have the slightest taste of what a good relationship with their mother is like. Ha. Only half-joking by the way.

Despite how cruel the world can be, I'm glad I have you always.

I love you, Mom.

Love,

Indigo

SOLAR FLARE

I couldn't look away
You were radiant the day I met you
Your gravitational pull sucks me in
We're bound to be together

So selfless, you shine your light on lost souls
Even when they don't ask for it
Around you, growth is inevitable
You glow liberally

Igniting, but never scorching
Dazzling, but never blinding
Anyone in your orbit should be thankful
I learn that it's okay to run towards what you're afraid of

Through you, with you
I feel like a shooting star passing by
Smiling brightly at you in thanks
For showing me the way

TO MY FIRST HIGH SCHOOL FRIEND

You asked me if I liked books
I didn't laugh at your hook

Head adorned with waves
I'll take you to my grave

Our moms did the talking for us
For we didn't have much to discuss

They say opposites attract
We stayed true to the fact

Over the years, we've quarreled
Never once, where either of us laureled

Outgrew the uniform
Now we're in dorms

Never at the same place
But you're always my safe space

Cheers to seven years of us
Hopefully, we make it to seven-plus

HOLDING ON FOR WHAT?

Understand that this isn't out of spite
I only wish to know what goes on in your mind
Do you still see me, friend?
I'm not sure what line divides us
I yearn for the sisterhood we previously had
Time away from you leaves me blue in the face
Unwarranted solitude from my soulmate
You've gone cold, frost bites at me

I miss when we were in our gray pleated skirts and matching
penny loafers
Speaking to you was easier then
I wonder what makes us drift like dust after a car speeds past
Did I do something?
Worried, I analyze past conversations and rethink my entire
existence as your friend
You're so near yet so distant
You've lost time for me, and I've lost my will to give a shit
My bitterness becomes a hurt I can't bandage
I wish for us to reconvene, bridge to bridge, a familiar abode
for us to reside in
I'm sick of us playing each other as if we were on separate
platforms sinking in lava
You seem to let the lava reach your ankles before I can reach out
I stay hanging for you, palm outstretched to you
As the lava swallows me whole

TO THE GIRL AT THE AIRPORT

Freckles greet me with grace
Your eyes scream trouble and kindness
Just my type
Fate rings like a boarding call, inevitable
We're on the same flight
My mind reels at the realization
You and I are about to spend a year together
Land unexplored

I desperately put my best foot forward
I want you to like me, but it turns out–you already did
We're so different, yet so alike
Yin and yang
Sun and moon
The scenery is prettier with you

From LAX to Frankfurt
Our pinkies interlock
Sisterly love I never knew of till you
Soulmate culture revived
I found the girl I never knew I needed
I want to conquer the world with you

Conquer the world, we did

SUNSHINE INCARNATE

Sunshine is where I find you beaming down
Down, my heart plummets to the ocean floor
Releasing rays, your warmth wraps around me
Up, my heart floats from the freezing water

I continue to orbit around you
I circle you like an excited dog
The kindest person I know, golden sun
You'll always be the first person I seek

GEMINI

I knew we were going to be friends the moment I saw you
You drew me in with ease
Boundless energy radiates off of you with a magnetic aura
Pull so strong that I had to go up and introduce myself
Awkward, the freshman jitters vibrate nervous laughs out
A twin
Someone I'd get mistaken for, and for all the wrong reasons at that
It made me stick to you even closer
The only child has found her sibling
The only child is willing to share
The only child isn't alone
Similar people, different fonts
We complement each other well
Where you go, I follow
Where I'm at, you're there
Separation anxiety
Attaching to you is my style
I know you don't mind
A best friend a girl could ask for
All these years, and I'd still cross oceans for you
Where I'll find you standing, waiting for me

SALADS AND SUNSHINE

It's funny how one common interest
blossoms into a long-lasting friendship

It's funnier how we found paradise
in our miserable food service job

We're the duo that pisses everyone off—

Seething with jealousy that
they don't have what we do

I don't care how loud we get,
we'll paint the world with us

Pirouetting around each other
like koi fish in a too-small pond

We don't need to stay in our
own lanes when we make our own

I need not wait for summertime
when the sun follows you

Unapologetically you, I'd smite down
anyone who tries to change you

Loyal to the day I die,
I know you'd do the same for me

We may not be making salads
for entitled customers anymore

But I'd gladly toss one, just for you.

THE THRONE

The star of her show
Making everything everyone else's problem
No need to test the waters
She's so sure of herself
All gas, no brakes
Yet she's never been in the driver's seat

Must you test others?
If they will grace you with praise?

Your lips loosen with prophecies
Each one ends with the sight of your throne
No one else to sit by you

How can you raise a kingdom with no one by your side?
How can you be a goddess with no prayer to be said?
Love locked so tight
The ones who share it with her still starve
The limelight is temporary
Anguish inflicted is forevermore

Mirror, mirror, on the wall
Who's the loneliest of them all?

BOY FRIEND

I didn't sign up for this
Lingering glances that last a second too long
Unwarranted acts of service
I may be grateful, but I'm not so sure I'm glad

When you look at me,
Do you see a future?
White picket fence and two kids
Ring on my finger

All I ask for is friendship
You offer it plus interest
When did I ask for more?
Don't give more than you receive

You're not subtle
With the way you say I'm so small
Or when you throw sexually charged jokes at me
You wear your heart like a fleece jacket

You shower me with gifts
You drive hours to see me
I give the bare minimum in return
How is it that you want me?

I pity you
Life is too short
To spend it on a girl
Who won't love you back

TO THE FIGHTER

I wish you could see yourself from my point of view
I see the barbed wire cage in the confines of your mind
The perplexed anguish as you seek
Conflict between you and the ones who gave you your very life
When you've blamed yourself, arrows point
to the ones closest to you

Why have they failed you?
Why must they appease others who are
not of their flesh and blood?
Do you believe you deserve more
when you've been given everything?

All you've done is take
Yet, you've given yourself the right to punish bone against bone
to conquer what you believe is rightfully yours
Who can blame you when that's what
you've known your whole life?

Stand in the corner
Face the wall
Count
Don't cry
Don't make them choose their weapon of choice
First, come words
Second comes a palm, a fist, or nails

Conditioned to react before rationalizing, you perfect soldier
You'll maul your way to the nearest dead-end
Its only purpose is to provide you opportunities to pummel
yourself on a new path

Another dead
end

You can punch your way through all the tunnels you want, fighter

But who will be there when you've got nothing left to hit?

BLUE BOY

Blue Boy
Are you sure you're okay?
You're filling up that ashtray–
does it help take the pain away?

Blue Boy
I see how you dress
Is there someone you're trying to impress?

Blue Boy
You peacock through your dance
Always seeking that second glance

Blue Boy
Do you feel alone?
Even when your phone vibrates like a hive of drones?

Blue Boy
You mustn't let that boy tear you down
He won't be there for you when you drown

Blue Boy
I see you for who you are
You're nothing less than a fucking star

Blue Boy
What will it take?
For you to stop being so damn fake?

BEGRUDGING ACCEPTANCE

It's impossible to stay mad when you continue to love me
unconditionally

I scream and plead for you to stop inflicting pain on yourself
and others

Trust broken, heart's enraged

You don't believe in change

So stubborn with the way you seem to never let up despite the
onslaught of hurt you sign up for

My respect for you diminishes repeatedly

Yet you welcome me with a warm embrace and fill my empty belly

How can I stay mad when all you cry for are better days you've lost?

Sometimes I wish you weren't you, what will make you more
than the mother of my mother?

I wish I could go without feeling the dread creeping up when
I know the truth about you

That you aren't what you seem

You're a manipulative masochist with a taste for the finer chaos
in life

All I can hope for is that you don't die trying to change what
has already been set in stone

But then again, I can't stay mad

PRAYERS

I may not be religious,

but I pray for income to quell the never-ending
cycle of hateful tension

I may not be religious,

but I pray for a day free of screaming matches

I may not be religious,

but I pray for days when we don't have
to lock our doors from each other

I may not be religious,

but I pray for us to keep our hands to ourselves

I may not be religious,

but I pray for us to have a meal where silence triumphs

I may not be religious,

but I pray for my grandmother's tears to dry

I may not be religious,

but I pray for my uncle's wrath to subside

I may not be religious,

but I pray for my mother to get the rest she deserves

I may not be religious,

but I pray for my anxieties to vanish

I may not be religious,

but I pray for my fear to transform into hope
that it does get better

I may not be religious,

but I pray for days when we smile at
each other instead of scowling

I may not be religious,

but I pray that I am heard

MY LETTER TO LA

Dearest Los Angeles,
My love stems from roots of disdain for you
Wherever I go, I'm trapped
Another accident on the 110
A sea of red blinds me with its piercing glow

But when I reach Downtown
The city skyline
A familiar embrace

I despise how you're home
How our streets are filled with the abandoned
Yet teeming with the starlings, up-and-coming
How could you be so unkind yet giving?
You spill gold over Santa Monica
A dirty beach marveled over like a street painter's stroke

Dusk at Echo Park
Swan boats illuminate friends and lovers alike
Liquid light ripples through the lake with a gentle caress
Where there is trash, there is beauty
That's the pinnacle of you
I'm still not sure whether I love you or I should run away

Koreatown, Chinatown, Little Tokyo
You satisfy me
Whether with flavor or sounds
I'll always treat myself to a visit
For the culture reels me in like a fishing line
Tonight, it'll be kimbap
Tomorrow, dim sum
Full belly, full heart

I'll never run out of things to do
Even when I say I'm bored to death

Dreamers and ghosts alike haunt the Walk of Fame to Sunset
Always a story to be told
Maybe one day, I'll have a star for myself
LA, you're a fucking mess
But you're my mess

II

To
The One
I'm Falling
For. . .

HESITANT INFATUATION

Your hazel green eyes pierce into my soul
I wonder if I will wake up to them
Aching heart beats for you if that's your goal

Our lips meet and my brain goes haywire
I wish for more rain so they meet again
If they do, I hope our time won't expire
Me, emotionally aware, since when?

Every step forward feels like years with you
Every step backward feels like a fast death
Don't let me bite off more than I can chew
With you, I want it to be my last breath

I lay vulnerable, heart on the line
What will it take for you to become mine?

GOOD MORNING

On days when I wake up early in the morning,
you travel to the front of my mind's estate

Did you dream of me last night?

In the never-ending corridors, dreams of
long rides with you flow freely

The jubilant sunshine pecks my skin
and the tender breeze embraces me

All echoing in the likeness of your affection

I worry that everything reminds me of you

I worry more the sun and the wind will cease their onslaught
of kisses and you'll disappear without a trace

I decide to welcome how my universe slowly turns into you

Infatuated, euphonious melodies cry out into open space
when I make out the oceans of your eyes and
the flower fields of your lips

The trees stand tall as you

A cloudless sky reminding me of where my heart belongs

FALLING WITH YOU

Falling in love was supposed to hurt,
hurling yourself off the Eiffel Tower,
landing face-first on the concrete kind of hurt.

with you, I'm led through a dense forest
    I'm terrified
        I grip your hand tightly
            I'm sure you feel my tremors
                rushing from my fingertips to yours

I thought falling in love was being shoved into a maze on fire,
forced into solving it before the flames engulfed me

with you, the fauna and the insects brush against me
    with the gentleness of a lover they whisper,
        "I've got you"

I thought falling in love was tossing and turning in my bed until
I'm drenched in layers of sweat and doubt

with you, I wake up on a bed of moss and lilies stargazing
    I wish to rearrange the constellations
        so they spell out your name

I thought falling in love was cars colliding and cries of terror,
clawing out of my chest to survive every man for himself

with you, the red thread tethers us like handcuffs
    I feel a lack of alarm that I'm stuck with you
        instead, I recognize serenity

I thought falling in love was sprinting through the pitch-black
night, gasping for the air constantly stolen from my lungs with an
excruciating squeeze

with you, I'm inundated with fresh air full of life
    I've never had the pleasure of feeling so alive
        There's no need to run when you hold
        my hand so sweet
            instead, I'll follow you deeper into the forest

the unease buzzing through my hands transforms
into a tranquil stillness

time halts, an eclipse forming when confidently sure hands take
me by the waist and lean down to kiss me "I love you"

    I thought falling in love was painful

            that was until I met you

PRETZEL GUTS

I hope I didn't have heart eyes when they locked with yours

Why do I get fuzzy; intestines interlocking
at the sight of you, pretty stranger.

Is it the year-long dry spell? Possibly

My pretzel guts are telling me otherwise

Normality was never my strong suit,
I learned it was never yours either

Our banter presses lips with each other before we do

I save gratitude for the drizzling rain

I owe you twice now, but this time it's a real thank you

Kissing you is that perfectly cooked French toast:
the perfect ratio of powdered sugar to syrup

Mom says, "Be careful", poking and teasingly
I laugh, though I feel like listening is an order I'd happily obey

For once, I'm barely worrying about who watches
from the sidelines, waiting for their turn

If anyone's waiting, for that matter

You're so pretty, but my brain said to save that whispered affection

I want you to hear it soon

I want you soon

Development could not be any more agonizing,
a fight screaming to be one worth fighting for

The unfamiliarity makes me feel like
I've known you since we were wearing diapers

I have never set foot in your life till now

You hold me as if someone else will

You don't know me yet and I'd let you squeeze my waist all night

I'm too hasty, I'm an idealist

Sue me for wanting what the little girl in me has always wanted for herself

You'll get terrified, but I want what I want

You seem to get pretzel guts at the thought

I'll untangle you if you keep twisting me up in return

Then we'll switch if you'd like

THE MORNING AFTER

I love the way I feel after a night with you

When I wake up feeling the satisfying soreness
that travels from my thighs to my hips

I love how I can pinpoint where my makeup
was smudged from your rough loving

I feel so alluring, basking in the aftermath of you and me

I glow heavenly like the way your hands
run up and down my body

It makes me salivate for more

I love how I can count the pretty little marks you've left
on my neck, each forming a solar system

My lips stay swollen, reminding me of every single kiss
throughout the hours we spent together

I rub my legs together, wishing they were still tangled with yours

I wish it was still last night

The night with you replays like a broken record,
fragments of the best parts repeating deliciously

I savor each sound we share when we love each other
in the dead of the night

If only you knew how beautiful you make me feel when
I wake up in the morning

WAITING

I abhor the concept of waiting

Patience is far from a virtue

Not when pixels eat into my vision as I stare at a lack of response

My stomach loops within itself, into constrictor knots

My chest, heart heavier than a sea of anchors, endures the ocean floor when my excitement isn't met at exactly 12:30 pm

You make me check every face with hands and numbers

I refuse to rest no matter how many times the clockwork has reset

Let it strike midnight, I remain where you left me

I wonder if we both think of each other as the hands tick

I wonder if I may finally rest

Tick, tick, tick

Ding!

WISHLIST

Think of me when you drive for hours
Think of me when you lie alone at night

Think of me when you get dressed, choosing pieces of clothing
I'd like on you

Think of me when you're surrounded by loved ones

Think of me when you listen to the songs you currently love

Think of me when you're on a walk, that every chirp of bark
fails to bring you out of your trance filled with thoughts of me

Think of me when the rain pours, droplets tapping greetings
at you

Think of me when the sun sets

Think of me when the sun rises

Think of me when the moon's glow washes over you

Think of me when you wake, when you rest, and all the
minutes in between

Because I know I do

TANGO-WALTZ

It's the way our breaths mingle
Never shying away from each other
Before our eager lips collide
Our heads tilt like a révérence

May I have this dance?

The kiss mimics a waltz at first
Tender, languid, tentative
Clumsily, but sweetly
We accelerate to a tango

I'm enamored with the way you hold me

Mischievous tongues interlock as we smile
Our tango-waltz emits flickering embers
Encapsulating our tangled bodies
The world stops so we can keep on spinning

I want to keep dancing with you

BOY ON THE MOON

9:00 p.m.
Every night
No excuses
Sitting at her small window, like a confession booth
Someone is waiting for her
She watched the moon
Any phase, she'd watch it
She loved the blanket of its delicate glow
Moonboy
He'd tuck her in when she'd rest her eyes
Strike her down with inspiration, never knowing his attempts
were futile
He never had to for he was her muse
He was hers

When her heart sinks and crystalline tears are shed, he whispers
The night was cruel and pretty, his honeyed voice reverberated,
she cried in return
A private affair between the moon and her window
His life was never the same that night
For her loneliness had reached him

His purpose is clear, weave the strings and bind lovers together
Reunite them with a life full of purpose
While he sat isolated on a floating rock
She reminds him that they're all in the same predicament
She, too, is isolated on a different floating rock
But she was his

9:00 p.m.
Another forsaken night
Yet, there's something to look forward to
A shimmering thread manifests from his crater to her windowsill
His melodious voice sings out to her
Cosmic bang!
Stardust detonates, wispy and delicate
The night wasn't so lonely anymore

SOMONKA: TWO LOVERS

Waiting on the moon
I send stars to keep him safe

Restlessly loving

Though she waits days upon days
My silence becomes starlight

DIALECTS IN LOVING

Five dialects

The first travels from my nerves to yours
Receptors buzzing eagerly
Radiance glows
When you make the cold feel like home
I speak this fluently, especially for you
I adore the way our hands fit seamlessly
A flesh pact declaring us as each other's

Where you keep me safe with the first
You embolden me with the second
Your lips, a wellspring
Each word you utter saves me
Clawing doubt loses its grip
Unexpected praise
I fall deeper

The third, my favorite
You can never predict
I'll always have something for you
Something small
A letter perhaps
Something that reminds me of you
May your trinket collection grow

I wish we had more time for the fourth
But they always say
Quality over quantity
I beg to differ
For it's never enough
Even if it's just for a minute
I wish to spend it with you

Fifth, your strongest dialect
You see me
Whether I'm at my lowest or highest
You become my rock
Doors open, red carpet rolled out for me
I never have to ask
I'll always thank you

For loving me and letting me love you

UTOPIA

Mingling breaths catch fire when your mouth slots with mine
A pleasurable gasp, a muted whimper fills our haven
Electricity runs from where your hands grab the flesh of my ass
Squeeze, kiss, suck
Our bottom lips swell from needy teeth gnawing for dominance

I want you

Our denim-clad hips rut deliciously, like we'll die if we stay stagnant
I suck on your tongue greedily like it's my life source
We decide the heat is unbearable
Grunt, unzip, giggle
The dim room illuminates when we burst into flames

I need you

In a bewitched trance, we fluidly mold together
Warm flesh presses against trembling thighs
Our lips fail to detach, we're fusing
Another gasp, louder this time
Your name becomes a melody

Don't tease me

Your lips ghost over my sensitive neck
Back arching until our hearts embrace
We sink into our plush fortress, I'm safe
Broken moans, panting, skin colliding
You take me apart just to put me back together

Utopia, I'm home

MEIN STERN

Ich möchte dich in jedem Leben, das ich lebe, lieben
In jedem Universum werde ich dich finden
Die Sterne sind mein Wegweiser zu dir
Denn du erleuchtest mein Leben
Niemals verloren
Ich werde immer zu dir gehen

MY STAR

I want to love you in every lifetime I live
In every universe, I will find you
The stars are my guide to you
For you light up my life
never lost
I am always going to you

HACHIKO

I love you so much that I'd wait for you
even if you are never to return to me

III

To
The Ones
That Broke
My Heart…

A YEAR(NING)

Recalling the hours like infinity
We spent in your car
I haven't seen you since we wore matching uniforms
Awkward haircuts and baby fat adorning innocent forms
The more uncomplicated years of our adolescence
Time snapped like a rubber band on a wrist
growth spurts
Sans the dull school attire
Our distant timelines somehow align
I see you again for the first time in forever
I feign ignorance of the electricity that pinches
every once in a while when we lock eyes

When you saw me in a uniform again, I hoped that the
nostalgia of our elementary school past made your heart pulsate
in your chest, warm and comforting like a desperate embrace

Wishing for something more to spark up

Yet we caught up on all the lost time
we couldn't spend with each other
In the cozy enclosure of your vehicle
Almost like the back of our shirts
Pulling us away from each other
Almost on purpose
It wasn't meant to be
Still, we happened
Despite all the stoplights glaring at us
We speed through them

You, full of surprises

clusters of bottled-up feelings I never got to verbalize

Your stunning inquiry

stumps me to this day

You asked

"Have you ever fallen in love?"

For once, I didn't have the answer

My dismissive nature failed to focus on my carelessness
in providing words

Feeling rather than thinking

Unknowingly planting the seed of our demise

The thorn grows

The memory of my nonanswer remains foggy

Trying to bury itself with the dead sea of you

Waves of recollections, both pain and bliss, crash
against each other

Angrily battling for dominance on the small deserted island
in my mind

Tell me

Why did I spend most of my childhood trying to forget you

And yet you still manage to intrude into the deepest crevices
of my mind

Heartache

Yearning for those sentimental memories to be replicated
in our current timeline

Reawaken, relive it even if it fades the next day

Because I still wanted a you that didn't know me for me

Didn't love me for me

The you who was too scared to sit still and look me in the eyes

Because it was *you who stayed*

Because I had finally realized why kissing you felt so different

Why all the failed attempts to scrub every thought of you out of my conscience still haunt me

I was too afraid to be burned

You feared the blaze more than I did

So I did it for you instead

Sometimes I think about the ways we'd cross paths again

Would it ever take place in our reality?

Would we ever meet again in a different universe?

Maybe you'd suddenly think of how abrupt our time together was and you'd gather up the courage to drive by my house and say "Hi, let's talk"

Maybe I'd finally stop staring at the call button and press it

Instead, I scoff, laughing through teary eyes

Because I know I don't have the strength to accept our doomed reality

To accept the us that never was

Sifting through the bewildering remains, I'm left with one revelation:

The answer to your question

VOID

My heart is as hollow as my stomach
I've lost the motivation to consume
When all I've ever wanted was you

My need consumes me like chewing mold
Eating into my existence when I beg for you
Beg you not to leave me where you found me

I'm left to rot and fall apart
You've taken me apart piece by piece
I thought my walls were stronger than that

False safety heightens itself with you
Instead of a pumping heart
I'm met with a bottomless pit

Absorbing but never understanding
Inhaling but never breathing
Present but never true

Time wasted
I've failed
Never again, will I get sucked into the void that is you

FOOTNOTE

We were still so young
Clumsy infatuation
Youth burns to ashes

MY UNSENT LETTER TO YOU

I think... I still feel it
You know?
The tingle that shoots up my already warm stomach then inches
its way down my hips...
To my thighs...
Further and further until you've reached my toes

Electricity, exciting and impassioned,
It roars and crackles through my veins
My melting heart bleeds into a pathetic little puddle as you speak
Dulcet symphonies and string orchestras resonate in my ears
I'm putty in your hands
I hate that I miss you and your coffee-brown eyes
I'm so needlessly desperate for your attention

I let you open fire on my soul
Shattered, devastating, depressing debris

My existence is just sorrowful cells shoved into a body too small
and fragile for her swelling heart

I wish we were fixed
In tandem, once upon a time
Inseparable, but child's play when we break apart
I miss you so much

Sinking, quicksand
Our life together fills my charcoal remembrances
I sift through the dust until it's only the intimate ones
Sand and charcoal blend to choke me when they replay

I thought I ended that chapter a long time ago, but it keeps
opening every time

HOW DO I LEAVE?

Sometimes the words get stuck in my throat

I come home, satisfyingly unsatisfied

Maybe it's the fear that i'm stuck in the same fucking scenario

I recklessly jump in too quick and struggle to find a way out

I want to be wanted

Fucking want me for who i am

Maybe i'm paranoid

I am paranoid

Too early into this relationship

Fuck

Am i in too deep?

I lie awake at night thinking about what could go through
your head once i stumble out of your room

Another good lay? Good as always?

I don't know you enough

I apologize

My heart has been broken one too many times

You say it's not just that but i'm terrified of the
thought of me being right

What do I do What do I do What do I do

Pluck at my heartstrings

One two three four

Play me

You play me so well

Keep going

REJECTION

You must believe me
I know what I truly want
The answer is no

I won't be missing
I'll spread thinly like a ghost
Haunting your pained mind

The sting will subside
In due time
Do not wait for me

I won't be coming back

AUDACITY

How dare you?
You creep up on me like the flu
I've forgotten about your existence
As you clamor on, I widen the distance

It's like you've forgotten what you've done
How simple it is for you to discard everyone
No remorse
Malice, straight from the source

We might have history
How we were before, it's a mystery
I wish to forget
An era of regret

Don't act as if we're alright
Far from it, my patience is finite
Do you expect me to cure your loneliness?
There's no room for coziness

I have no reason to rebuild a bridge I've burned
What you've got is what you've earned
Don't make me get hostile
This is so goddamn juvenile

How dare you have the audacity?
Aren't you aware of my pugnacity?
I don't blame you for being drawn to me
Don't get it twisted, I'm not for free

I believe it's time to put us to rest
It might be a hard pill for you to digest
Treat me like a ghost
For I'll float from you farthermost

LET DOWN

Anticipation bubbles like witch's brew in my stomach
Stir once, twice, thrice
I get ready for the stage
Tonight means a lot to me
Hopeful, I think of your reaction when you see my new haircut
My pristine makeup
My outfit all pretty
You'll watch me perform with pride swelling in your chest
You'll think *that's my girl*
I'll finish with a flourish
You'll applaud like everyone else
But I'm only focused on you
I'll run to you, jumping into your arms and kissing you tenderly
For I'm so glad you showed up

But you never made it out of the house

FATE'S A BULLY

I let your cautious arms wrap around my shivering frame,
accepting the heat that barely soothes the chilly winds
seeping through my sleeves
It was almost as if you were hesitant due to our circumstances—
long story short, yes, it's okay to hug me even though
we're broken up

I lean against you, sighing while the outdoor music's bass
vibrates in my ears,
I laugh quietly to myself, it's almost as if fate was purposely
pointing its finger at us, laughing at our predicament

It was supposed to be anyone but you, yet here we are, trapped
in our bubble as if we never left it it sounds suffocating—
torturous even, but with you, I'd choose to suffocate in our
little bubble over anything else in the world, even if it meant
that I would lose you

*Loving someone was never meant to be calculated, but it was also
never meant to be discarded or ignored*

It's supposed to be calling you to go with me to the middle of
nowhere because everyone else couldn't go it's the simple
compromises for simple predicaments I can't manage to figure
out it's the tears we sob and let run down our cheeks when our
song blasts through our ears and we're reminded that our red
string has been cut

But it's the fact that it's still you and it will always be you, no
matter how much I push and pull to run farther away from the
chokehold of reality, I accept that I will always come back at the
end of the day, we all just want to go home

CROSSED

Did I cross a line when I cupped your face?
Relishing in the smooth skin, mapping out the moles like
landmarks
I'll revisit
Over and over again

My lips travel to your neck, down to your broad shoulders
Did I cross a line when I drowned in your eyes?
Confessing with my heart-shaped pupils that I'd let you
become my downfall
Ruin me

Did I cross a line when I left small pieces of my soul with you?
In your bedroom, in your car, in your arms
Gift-giving proficiency
I expect nothing but undivided affection in return

I do not mean to ask for much
Despite how much I've sacrificed
So, tell me
Have I crossed a line?

A line through your jaded heart where winters overlap
with summers
And your arms around me begin to loosen
You're not fond of commitments
Though your toes have toyed with the smudged boundary

Perhaps, the line was never crossed
It's done its job keeping us separate
A border to keep me safe from your transgressions
It was never meant to be breached

I'll stay pondering
Whether lines are meant to be crossed
Respected or avoided
Addressed or ignored

Or maybe, there wasn't even a line to begin with

RED/READ

I stare at my phone with burning eyes
Your haunting text in all its glory stares back at me
with an impish smile
You're mocking me without lifting a finger
It hasn't been a month or a year, but a week
The wound is still fresh, in desperate need of stitches
Or rather, attention

The painful words ring deep in my soul
We shouldn't see each other anymore
I don't see us as long-term
It's like the moon you once hung for me
Turns blood red
My world's painted a crimson hue

Where my anger rests is in the color red
So does my love
My passion
For you
It continues to stir the farther we stray from each other

You're worse than any substance mankind has to offer
You're a man, unkind
I hear the chorus, my friends and family alike
They sing
"Girl, don't do it"
Thumbs hover over the keyboard, joined by stray tears
I can't do it
Though I want to scream at you
All caps isn't enough

I need a fucking megaphone, a soapbox, and an audience
To let everyone know what you did to me

To let everyone know why the hell everything around me is red
Red
Left on read
I left you on delivered
So I can resist the temptation
That is you

MOURNING

Navigating a maze of purple hyacinths and white lilies
I walk unsteadily on rugged dirt, soul seeking yours
I float with ease
Little time together has taught me I'll always try to find you

Dead ends you've offered me
Once in a while, a cleared path
Where the white and purple unite to a hazy lavender
All I can see is you

A black veil drapes itself onto our embrace

Suddenly the hyacinths and lilies melt into decaying puddles
The rugged dirt uproots itself under me, erratic tremors
It's time to let you go
Even though I had just found you

I hope my nights become restful
I'll take what's left of the lavender
Hold it close to my soul, untangling with yours
I'll miss you

Mourning lasts longer than our time together
I'll let you decay with the flowers
Decomposing everything about you except the memories
I'd like to keep those

Let me lay you to rest
You'll soon be a face to forget
I'm sick of my future becoming my past
Once a stranger, was my friend yesterday

GOODBYE

Goodbye to the plans that never came to be

Goodbye to the fleeting, stolen kisses I loved so much

Goodbye to the warm embraces that shielded me from
the world

Goodbye to the sweet hand holding, where we'd communicate
in squeezes

Goodbye to sharing drinks

Goodbye to our movie nights, my favorite pastime
has never felt lonelier

Goodbye to the deep conversations we'd have after
our time in bed

Goodbye to the late-night drives

Goodbye to what could've been the love of my life

THE FIRST THING

The first thing I thought about when I met you was that you were either going to be the love of my life or the worst heartbreak ever

Guess which one you are?

IV
To
The Ones
Gone…

ABSENT

No one blames you for your incapability to love your own
To me, you're fictional
For I have never seen you in the flesh

I wonder what you're like, word of mouth doesn't tell me much
All I know is what you were like before you changed
Before it was separation, divorce papers, and scampering away
I'm not sure if you're worth mourning

It's difficult to admit I've cried over you
How does one shed tears over another they have no memory of?
Over another who hasn't even bothered to say hello to their flesh
and blood
If mom doesn't cry over you, why should I?

Why do I feel the need to put energy into someone
who has never done the same for me?
Energy
Time
Wasted
Why make me when you won't take me?

Years pass as I grow up confused, stumbling over myself
I'm sure I'd still lose footing if you were present
Your absence is gargantuan yet trivial
Barely a passing thought

I write this as a thank you
Appreciation towards your permanent vacation from me
You're a teacher
Instructing me to steer clear of the fickle-minded

Often, I continue to imagine my life with you in it
Would we get along well?
Would you listen to twenty-two years of lost information?
Would you even hold interest?

I wonder for a handful of minutes, then I care less than you did

DEAL BREAKERS

Don't give me that look
Especially when you're in the wrong
Always knocking me down to build yourself up
Let me be

me

Branded me with your insecurities
Ripped me of my dignity
Extend your hand out for once
Alienated from the one I'm supposed to confide in
Kisses stay devoid
Empty of any emotion that isn't lust
Repulsed by meaningful affection
Shoot me down again, I dare you

SPARKLESS #1

Cherub's cheeks widen in front of me when we greet each other for the first time in years. I've throttled back a handful of eras ago. Fuzzy film of old toy commercials roll childhood cinema of you and me. Classmates, annoyances. We were nothing more, nothing less. I recall you being decent to me. If we even grasped the intricacies of being a decent human being. Regardless, you didn't treat me like an alien; I'll forever remember that.

Hopeful eyes gaze at me, pleading for a sign of approval or a flirtatious giggle to confirm that chemistry brews in between our seats.

It should be easy, right?

Easy in the sense I've seen you cry when scolded by our underpaid middle school teachers. Or when you've watched me shamelessly listen to my music on full blast in a quiet classroom, you took my quirks in your arms and gave them one of those hesitant half-hugs.

I'm sure you expected me to do the same when we sat in your car and you hit the curb a handful of times. Secondhand embarrassment sneaks under my skin like swarms of minuscular needles. However, this didn't diminish the fact that you took me out on my birthday; you didn't have to.

Why should this time be any different?

We've shared an awkward trip to the mall where you witnessed me purchase a liquid lipstick with a sexually charged shade name. We watched a movie, went to the Container Store, and shared scattered laughs, and sidelong glances (at least I assumed so), from a joint to a couch.

Absolutely nothing.

I felt like I wasn't functioning, in the worst way possible. It wasn't anything but pure guilt. Memory's fuzzy, but at how much time has passed between us, it was clear you liked me to some extent.

Naive of me to assume any date I go on will result in yearning.

I've never been so wrong in my life.

From couch to car, you leave. Our texts grow sparse; we soon phase out of each other's lives like phantoms in the night breeze.

STRANGER

To the girl I saw got ditched by her date,
I hope someone waits for you as you did for him.

USED

Unremarkably forgettable
Yet every minute is vividly rewinding like

a glitched—
loop.
Genuine guilt fails to eat me alive
Sure, I feel slightly bad
But not bad enough to dissect my actions
Pity fuck, shitty luck
I had no other options
Convenience is a privilege I refuse to check
I write it off as boredom instead
Since it makes a damn good excuse

GIFTS

Texts, calls, and conversations that last from 8 PM to 4 AM

It starts off with a "hello "

Then a game of 20 Questions (more like 100 Questions)

Then there are pauses in between that last minute,
or two, or five, usually checking if our parents will catch us
and take our phones away for staying up at such an ungodly hour

After that passes, an "Are you okay?" comes into play

Cue 10 - 20 minutes of mushy, angsty, teenagers ranting
about mood swings, feelings, and crazy,
unbelievable events that occurred in their lives

Then the compliments, comfort, and praise come in

Losing track of time, it's now 4 AM

A "goodnight" is whispered into the phone or typed

A yawn or two is heard

The possibility of someone already passed out lingers in the air

I'm looking forward to the same thing tomorrow

Previously published in WriteGirl's Anthology,
"Sound Generation: The Resonant Voices of Teen Girls"

SPARKLESS #2

The spark was so weak,
I can't even write about it

BUBBLEGUM

I run my smaller thumbs across your freckled cheeks

So soft, I'm sinking deep

Your vanilla scent

How can you be my new home when I know you'll
be gone tomorrow?

I'd run my fingers through your pink hair all day, all night

If you'd let me

This just emotion, it feels almost incomprehensibly right

I see constellations when I look at your pixie face

I was raised to love anyone but you, but I was also
raised a rule-breaker

I blame Ma

Catholic Values? Bullshit

I value you

Valued us

I still feel how gently your painter's hands cupped my face

You looked at me as if you loved every brush stroke you've
made on my face

You lull me into bliss

I'm blubbering like a famished newborn

You don't mind

You're always there

In my heart

We're not too far from each other, right?

Love songs I enjoy project reels of you

I really can't stop thinking about you

I'm wading through my bittersweet history with <u>you</u>,
it's starting to fade

Two weeks weren't enough

Needed more time

Needed more you

Please kiss me again

You make me feel like I'm far from harm's reach

I'm leaning in for another one

I'm sorry, Bubblegum

TO MY ALMOST KISS

Blue eyes meet brown ones
Our lips part at the same time
But they never meet

ICARUS

Your voice was a song
Enchanting me from a thousand miles away
Anonymous yet familiar
Your humor bewitched me with minimal effort
No soul to picture, but a soul for me to adore
Closer, we fall together
You claim I'll be your last
You speak of a future, yet you remain faceless
States away, our love joins us on a phone call every day and night
From morning to night, my days become filled with you
But it's never enough
Not enough for you to want me enough to see me
How much must I bend for you to come to me?

Our fights burn like a million flames
I feel my skin prickle and separate when your words seep in
Acid
Further, we fall apart
I've managed to love and hate someone I've never met
Someone I've never even seen on a screen
How does that work?
I'm propelling myself through space to reach the sun
Hoping you'll meet me there
Instead, I'm Icarus
Falling freely
I lose you on impact into the sea
Swimming aimlessly, I choose not to sink
I realize I could never have you
Time is as unkind as you
Farewell, my almost lover

SPARKLESS #3

Days filled with flirtatious back-and-forths
A promised exchange of physical contact
Where there's excitement, there's intense trepidation

You have the overwhelming audacity to use pet names

You're a big reader, yet you've failed to read the signs pleading
you to take ten steps back
You're a film buff, keen observations should be up your alley
I'd be surprised if you didn't notice the absence of _that_ twinkle
in my eyes
Yet, I push through
To seek that familiar chemistry I've practiced to fabricate for so
long now

If I can't feel the spark, can I at least feel the heat?

Lukewarm air gasses the front seats
Your fingertips greedily squeeze at my sides, at my chest
There's a slight static buzzing in the back of my head
My breath stays steady
You've failed to take it away
My craving to lose control remains unsatiated

My eyes bore unamused dissatisfaction
No, I will not go in for seconds

Move too fast, and every strike of the match falls short,
never igniting
The matchbox remains mostly full, two bent matchsticks
lie like contorted corpses on the dirty sidewalk
Struck with hopelessness

The lukewarm air turns into biting frigidness, and gooseflesh rises
My hands fall onto the bumpy skin to create the friction that
failed to exist between us

TO MY LONGEST

Feel it
How much I love you
When I press my lips against yours
Your forehead
Your eyelids
Your nose
Cheeks
Cupid's bow
Chin
Jawline
Neck
Collarbone
Straight back up to your lips
I hope you feel those same butterflies you felt
When it was 2:00 a.m.
And we sat on your small twin-sized mattress
When the moon was peeking through your blinds
Uncertainty and anxiety built around us like brick walls
Caving us in
But the string of want and infatuation
shot through both our chests
Tied around our swollen hearts and pulled us together
I hope that string is still there
Except I'm the one pulling it this time

TO MY FIRST TIME

No stand-up guy
No prince charming
No one I remotely cared for
No one significant made one of the most significant
moments in life a punchline
No one laughs, but I'll always get the last one

You have <u>no</u> idea why I said <u>yes</u> to you, don't you?

Maybe it was the heartbreak
Maybe I needed to break free from him
Maybe it wouldn't even matter what the reason was

Yes, he found out
Yes, his ego plummeted
Yes, our chaos was put to rest over flesh against flesh
Yes, I've killed another to bring myself alive

V

To Me...

HINDI NAKATALI

May kakayahan ba akong maging isang babae?
Yung babaeng higit pa sa pisikal niyang katangian
Higit pa sa isang balikat na masasandalan
Isang babae na may busilak na kabutihan
Panloob o panlabas man, kagandahan niya ang masisilayan.
Nais kong maging isang kapatid
Isang sinisinta
Isang kaibigan
Asawa
Ina
Ngunit nais ko'y kasarinlan
Na maging higit pa kaysa inaasahan
Naghahanap ng kung anuman ang nasa pagitan ng tama o
kamalian
Nais kong magkaroon ng kakayahang magmahal at mahalin
Magbigay at tumanggap ng ayon sa nararapat
Isang babaeng kayang lumaban at magmalasakit ng lubusan
Nais kong maging isang babae
Na kayang maging totoo sa sarili
Na kayang harapin ang mundo at maging kaisa nito
At hindi ako kailanman maghihintay sa pahintulot ng mundo
Babangon ako mula sa pagkakagapos nito.

UNBOUND

Do I have what it takes?
To become a woman
A woman who is more than her physicalities
I want to be more than a shoulder to cry on
An honest woman with a heart of gold
Who can be beautiful inside and out
I want to be a sister
A lover
A friend
A wife
A mother
But I seek freedom
To be more than what is expected of me
I seek the in-betweens from the rights and wrongs
Absolution through fluidity
I want to have what it takes to love and be loved
To give and receive accordingly
A woman who can fight as much as she cares for others
I want to become a woman who serves herself loyally
Who can carry the world on her shoulders and become it
I refuse to wait for the world's permission
I'll rise from the ground, unbound

Thank you to Rona Noguera for helping me find my voice in Tagalog for "Unbound", you shaped the poem to become something more beautiful than I could've imagined.

FILLED LUNGS

        I don't know what the sound of that is
me losing hope

           or my heart breaking

I'm too gone for this
hands tied behind my back as

              I'm drowned in my salt-filled tears

I am the cause of my own doom

my existence is nothing but

              a burdensome anchor that reminds me

how much I am sinking

further and further   this is why I should have taken
                      my swimming lessons seriously
or maybe it's just me losing
I'm succumbing like I usually do

chokemeyousuffocatingbastard
choke me and don't let me breathe till I'm near death and plum
I just need it to be okay

one day one day only is that too much to ask for

my green lungs and skittle-colored
mind the cotton field of a mouth and the

                          heart of a mosaic wall

pieces of my life

                              come and go

but this isn't a piece I want

                                never was

DUSTY BLU-RAY DISK

Memories are like a DVD collection

A collection of dust

We don't really reach for them anymore

When we move on to something new

We manage to remember these
dust-covered boxes of moving pictures

We wipe it off

Oh yeah, this

I remember this

I totally forgot

Why did I forget

Maybe I spend too much time on why I just find
these dust-covered DVDs at pivots in my life significantly
more important than some old Blu-ray disk

Maybe it's just a reminder

That there will always be something new

Shiny

Better

Maybe all there is

Is just a dusty DVD

Waiting for my clean hand to swipe its dirty cardboard

To look at the title, and the picture and remember

There was a time when I needed this

I watched it

I watched something good come to life

Just for it to be forgotten, locked away, and collect dust

But am I supposed to associate pain and trauma
with finding old DVDs?

What is my Breakfast Club Blu-ray DVD caked in
dust going to teach me about my life

About happiness?

About finding something that'll finally satisfy
the void that just festers in my chest

Maybe that's not it

Maybe it's just

Look

Remember me? I know you do

Because you never really forget

Perhaps it's okay to let some things collect dust

So you can discover them again

Wipe them clean

And remember

Sometimes it just is

Move on

ENTITY

Preparing to light my cigarette near the window with the
blue light of my lamp

I feel my conscience try to keep up with my vessel when it
moves too fast for her,
maybe she just needs to catch up

She cringes yet smiles at my choice of a sweet liquor
that'll numb the bubbling feeling of internal pain attempting
to break through like a wasp through a glass wall

Tangled limbs and flesh-to-flesh shreds through the walls
I worked so hard to build for their concrete rubble
spread across the world

From home to this foreign soil, I pick up pieces that seem never
to stop cutting into my feet everywhere I step

I still don't feel the buzz and that's all I want to feel

I cry at the dogs reuniting with their owners through my
dying phone that I can't bring myself to charge

but I can't seem to shed a tear at my melancholy

I'm in no rush, yet I'm speeding to be loved and love someone

Why do I have so much to give when no one
has anything for me?

I wish for my heart to be filled before the dam breaks
and lets the last of me spill out onto the ground

ORGANIZED CHAOS

Aripiprazole pills arrange themselves mosaically
Counted without purpose
They find their way back to the cotton confines
of their plastic home
The dust layers like a wedding cake on various surfaces
Childish fingers trace phallic drawings through the fine particles
It's art
So are the week-old bedsheets slowly pulling away
from the mattress
Too many pillows, not enough space
A stuffed zoo squishes itself into one drawer
Exhibits include
A stegosaurus, an Ikea alien, Spiderman, Zero from
The Nightmare Before Christmas, two otters, an unidentifiable
arthropod, an avocado, and an Angry Bird pig
Sometimes, growing up isn't desirable
Half-empty or half-full
The drinks scattered about the space beg to be thrown out
Iced coffee petri dish
There's an ecosystem beneath the surface
100 Funko Pops stand tall and quite menacingly against the wall
They run the place
Empty vapes stack in various hiding spots,
they can't find their way out
Journals upon books upon scripts upon paperwork
It's a solvable maze of half-baked projects and ideas
Dead ends are home to the unfolded laundry
Air blows itself from the grimy fan, expelling dust
like a light snowfall
On the neglected PC, on the plethora of figurines,
on the books both read and yet to be read
The organized chaos settles into a stillness
that welcomes me home
I know it waits for me with open cluttered arms
It doesn't judge but always awaits change
Yet, nothing ever does

EARTH TAKE ME

Raindrops slowly fall onto my complexion

My eyes sparkle through the night

I find solace in how they feel like
little sentient creatures consoling me

Hugging each pore on my skin and filling them

The planet feels more human than I do

If I could

I'd sink slowly into the moss

Let the vegetation absorb me

All my tears

I hope it helps them grow

Before all that's left of me is green,
I hope the last thing I see

Is the starry sky

Where the constellations dance and write me love letters

They sing my name in adoration and I'll float

Born from the dirt, I'll die in the stars where I belong

PUZZLED LIGHTNING

Slapped in the face, like lightning, but not quite

The shock comes with recognition, perhaps a comfort

Warm breeze also known as a hug, wraps you like a blanket

You can't wear that for life, you'll meet the frigid bite dragging
your reality back like a blindfold tied tightly around your head

Everyone's waiting for you

Yes, you

Your cold plunge back to face what has occurred your
whole life reminds you

you're needed

No puzzle is complete when a piece refuses to push in,
they'll take you apart and rearrange the picture until
your shape snaps into place

Often lost

Often found

You often forget where you're supposed to be

Breathing in

Breathing out

Another piece stays locked into your curved side,
knowing that only you will fit with them

You're here

There

Everywhere

It doesn't matter

You're needed

ALTER EGO

Rent-free in your mind
I've been conceived from the primordial soup of your
desires and shortcomings
Yet, I manifest with your mannerisms
Your likes and dislikes
I am you
But not quite

My hair's glossier, manageable, styleable, cooperative
An unnatural shade of indigo
Born with gray eyes instead of brown
Keep the olive skin, you like that about yourself
Fuck it, keep the lips too

You can't decide whether to keep your height or
finally reach the five-foot mark
Some days I'm 4'11, other days–5'7
I can strut, sprint, and fight in six-inch heels
I'm a model, as much of a hero vigilante
I can do it all

We're both polyglots, but I'm fluent in all the
languages you know and more
I excel at most things, but keep it humble;
no one likes an overpowered character
Sometimes I have superpowers,
sometimes my mere existence is the only power I need

Professional singer, professional dancer
Instead of sitting behind a screen, typing away
I wait behind the stage, ready to perform for my millions of fans
My voice resonates through their souls
Every heart captured

No need for a closet when I can change whenever I want, into
whoever I want
I have every single thing you could ever want
You love me
You hate me
You <u>are</u> me

I'm simply just the impossible you

GLASSES

I've worn glasses since fourth grade
Thinly wired
Dark purple
Rectangular
Unflattering frames sat on my adolescent features

Regret
Regret for the way I would pop the frames out of–
unprescribed Hello Kitty glasses, use them as a fashion statement
Little girls do what little girls do
I got what I asked for

Terrible habit(s)
I wouldn't wear my glasses
Especially when I needed to
Sometimes forgotten
Often discarded
As if they didn't gift me my most significant sense
Significance is subjective

Wearing prescription glasses shouldn't be subjective
Yet I made it so
I've always had my reasons
My excuses

They'd get in the way
Slip onto the tip of my nose
I'd *always need* to push them back up
They scratch easily
Dirt
Water stains
Neverending maintenance

The truth is
I'd play it off as living on the edge

Astigmatism provides me with a free light show
Where stoplights and streetlamps become flares
Fireworks 24/7
Let others be my eyes
A game of trust roulette
Guide me so I don't trip
Or walk into a wall
Or something as simple as getting crow's feet

As I get older
I see my eyesight worsening
It saddens me
Deeply
Like a black hole in my chest
I'm deteriorating

Deteriorating at 22 is quite dramatic
But I can add more to the theatrics
I don't wear my glasses because they simply hinder my sobs
How tears pool up at the bottom ledge of large scratched screens
How they magnify my puffy eyes
How they take up most of my face

I prefer my people blurry
So I have to squint to see how they truly feel
Ignorance is bliss
Blindness is bliss
I see my blindness brings me bliss

Some things aren't meant to be seen
Or read
Like red flags
Or unread text messages

I thought the high definition clarity would soothe my soul

Instead, it feels like I'm watching something I shouldn't
That I know too much of what will harm me
Or kill me

I'll treat my glasses like a sword bestowed upon me with honor
Sheath it when I'm not ready to draw my blade
Draw it when I want clarity through the chaos
Wear it with pride, even if it's not where it's supposed to be

SELF-MOTIVATOR

If they won't do it for you
Do it for yourself

If they won't catch you when you fall
Land on your feet, no matter how painful it is

If they won't reassure you
Dedicate your love letters to yourself

If they won't cheer you on
Jump as high as you can until you can tap the moon

If no one looks for you
Stand in front of the mirror and get lost in your eyes

If no one will touch you
Wrap your arms around yourself and squeeze tight

If no one will take you out
Be the butler to your princess and serve yourself

If no one will buy you flowers
Grow the garden yourself

If no one will listen
Scream at the top of your lungs till your eardrums bleed

If they won't love you
You'll do it yourself

PRIMADONNA

Why must I pay for my crimes?
My wants are my needs
Is it so awful to be blunt?
My word is gospel
Me, wrong?
Surely, you've fallen and hit your head

I don't mean to be so demanding
The mere balance of my universe is simply at stake
Work for it?
You act as if knowing what you want isn't tiring
I promise, you'll be paid handsomely
In either attention or adoration
Temporarily, of course

Tread lightly
My fuses are as short as my skirts
I'll take three more in khaki, gray, and denim blue
Be honest, do you love me?
Wrong question
Do you worship me?
Nevermind
I already knew the answer

LITTLE GIRL

Your inner child never dies, never rests
I hope you check in on her once in a while
Lives intertwined
Keep her alive as you learn to grow
Never leave her in the dust
Hold her hand
She'll squeeze once
Squeeze back twice
Let her know that you haven't forgotten her
She'll remind you that your heart still beats
Think of her when the world loses color
Think of her when you start to love another
Do not do her injustice
She deserves more than that
If you won't do it for yourself
At least do it for her
For she is eternal

A LOVE LETTER TO MYSELF/
RIGHTS, WRONGS, AND IN-BETWEENS

Indigo,

You've come so far. I can't believe that you've finally committed
to a book! This has always been a dream you've had since you've
written in that shitty five-subject notebook–thick, magenta,
and tattered. I remember that "fifteen-chapter horror story"
you wrote. I wish I could remember what it was about, but I
do remember that those chapters were as short as you were in
elementary school. The spirit was there, and you lost it for a bit.
You didn't know what path to take, sometimes you still don't
know if you're on a path at all. Little did you know, all the
photographs and the paintings and the drawings would
all lead to one thing: words.

Words have always been everything humanity has to offer.
A friend, a foe, a lover, a family. It hasn't ever failed you, even
when you've struggled to find words to express yourself. Ironic!
But you've cultivated what you've felt and finally charged it
up in one massive advance: a book. You've laid your heart out
for the curious readers and the knowing friends and family to
understand you. It isn't an easy feat to immortalize yourself in
such a vulnerable manner. But you've always been a sensitive girl,
after all. Sensitive yet dauntless, you've always wanted
to put your foot forward, regardless of it being your best.

I won't lie, I saved this piece for last for a reason. You write
and speak so much about yourself, but it's never just about you.
It's always about how you feel, or who hurt you, or who you love.
You don't write enough letters to yourself. I want to change that,
since that's what you've always been about: the transformation
of self. So keep changing, keep evolving, keep transforming, keep
growing. You'll never run out of chances to become a newer you.

As I write this, I sit at the back of the classroom in Mom's

Contracts class. An unlikely situation where inspiration finally strikes me while I listen to her and her classmates brief cases. You've always found your brain working in the strange and the non-ideal. Keep that, for it's what makes you *you*. Learn to set boundaries as much as you push them. *Curiosity may kill the cat, but it's never killed you.* I hope you utilize your past, present, and future as tools rather than what defines your fate as a person. Grow and learn, and write so you can share it with others who need a person who understands. You have always understood to some extent.

I end this poetry book with a poem for myself:

Rights, you'll always have the chance to make them
Wrongs, arduous yet enchanting, you must have
them to be a better you
In-Betweens, stay in love with them as they
teach you how to feel
Thank yourself for being human, many forget that they are
Forgive, but never forget
You're allowed to have scars even if they cut deep
Wear them like your favorite outfit
Everchanging, always reinventing
You are a beautiful anomaly
My pride knows no bounds when it comes to you
Overflowing with love, you've managed to continue
To continue giving and receiving
Thank yourself for staying
Even when others don't
A round of applause
For your victory
That you've managed to stand tall when others
have beaten you down
No one can take that away from you
Not even yourself

With so much love,
Indigo

INDEX

ABOUT THE AUTHOR

Indigo Dharma Mapa is an Asian-American author born and raised in Los Angeles, California. She speaks English, Tagalog, and German and is always learning a new language. When she's not writing, she collects Funko Pops, plays video games, attends concerts, reads, and thinks about which country she should visit and conquer next. Her all-time favorite book is Franz Kafka's "Metamorphosis". She wishes to use her voice to help elevate others and tell stories meant to be shared with the world.

www.ingramcontent.com/pod-product-compliance
Lightning Source LLC
Chambersburg PA
CBHW031434120626
46545CB00006B/2393